MW01591156

1

THE TRUTH

ABOUT

HEAVEN

Questions Answered

By
Christine Pocza Backus

TABLE OF CONTENTS

Emanuel Lutheran Church
Tawas City, Michigan

This book is dedicated to my Christian parents who brought me to baptism and nurtured me in the Word, and to the Lutheran Schools I attended from first grade through my first and only year of college.

God is good and has blessed me beyond measure in both good times and sad.

I am eternally grateful!

EVERY KNEE SHOULD BOW!

Your attitude should be the same as that of Christ Jesus: Who, being in very nature God, did not consider equality with God something to be grasped, but made himself nothing, taking the very nature of a servant, being made in human likeness.

And being found in appearance as a man, he humbled himself and became obedient to death - even death on a cross!

Therefore God exalted him to the highest place and gave him the name that is above every name, that at the name of Jesus every knee should bow, in heaven and on earth and under the earth, and every tongue confess that Jesus Christ is Lord, to the glory of God the Father (Philippians 2: 6-11).

HEAVEN
Introduction

Then I saw a new heaven and a new earth...I saw the Holy City, the New Jerusalem, coming down out of heaven from God... The wall [of the city] was made of jasper, and the city of pure gold, as pure as glass. The foundations of the city walls were decorated with every kind of precious stone... [Jasper, Sapphire, Chalcedony, Emerald, Sardonyx, Carnelian, Chrysolite, Beryl, Topaz, Chrysoprase, Jacinth and Amethyst]. The twelve gates were twelve pearls, each gate made of a single pearl. The great street of the city was of pure gold, like transparent glass (Revelation 21:1, 2, 18-21).

Then the angel showed me the river of the water of life, as clear as crystal, flowing from the throne of God and of the Lamb down the middle of the great street of the city. On each side of the river stood the tree of life, bearing twelve crops of fruit every month. And the leaves of the tree are for the healing of the nations. No longer will there be any curse. The throne of God and the Lamb will be in the city and his servants will serve him. They will see his face, and his name will be on their foreheads. There will be no more night. They will not need the light of a lamp or the light of the sun, for the Lord God will give them light. And they will reign forever and ever. (Revelation 22: 1-5)

People have many questions about Heaven. Is it a real place? How do we get there? What will it be like? Will everyone go there when they die? Will we be reunited there with family members? Will we still be a "family"? Will we eat? Will we work? Will there be animals, and if so, will our pets be there?

Some years ago, on December 20, 2005, to be exact, ABC aired a documentary news special about Heaven. I was (not surprisingly) disappointed after watching this special because it offered no hope for people. In fact, in many ways it led people away from heaven rather than toward it. In this documentary Barbara Walters interviewed people from all walks of life.

The four main questions posed were:

1.   "Is there really a Heaven?"
2.   "Where is Heaven?"
3.   "How do we get there?"
4.   "Will everyone go there?"

At that time an ABC news poll reported, "Nine out of ten Americans believe that there is a Heaven and that they will go there when they die." Those statistics are still very much the same today (2020).

After watching this special I was amazed and astounded at the things people believe about Heaven. I was disappointed that most people, even members of the clergy, seem to believe and teach that we must earn heaven by being good and doing good things for God and our fellow human beings.

It makes my heart sad to see people being misled. In response I have, with the help of God and Scripture, tried to answer more clearly and truthfully the questions people have about heaven. We will never be able to completely comprehend what to expect in heaven until the day we as faithful believers are called home. But we do know from Scripture that it will be amazing and perfect. In the meantime, let me help you put your mind at ease by passing on to you the truth about heaven from Scripture.

IS THERE REALLY A HEAVEN?

The verses which I quoted at the beginning of this book from Revelation tell us that there indeed is a heaven.

Jesus refers to heaven when He tells His disciples, *in my Father's house are many rooms; if it were not so I would have told you. I am going there to prepare a place for you. And if I go and prepare a place for you, I will come back and take you to be with me that you also may be where I am* (John 14: 2, 3).

God does not reveal to us everything about heaven, possibly because it is beyond our comprehension. Rather, He speaks to us figuratively and uses comparisons which we can relate to. He describes it as a place of "many rooms". In the old King James version of the Bible John 14:2 reads, *In my Father's house are many mansions...* In Revelation 21: 1 we are told that at the end of this age there will be a new heaven and a new earth, and a city of gold and precious gemstones. Because we understand that gold and precious gems are beautiful, God uses those examples to help us visualize it and understand that it is an unbelievably awesome place.

Try to picture in your mind a street paved in gold, or a city gate made of a single pearl. I can't imagine a pearl that size, but it certainly would be beautiful beyond belief. What about the *river of the water of life, crystal clear and flowing from the throne of God*? And the throne of God will be much more beautiful than any throne of kings or queens we have ever seen or imagined in this life.

There are places here on earth where we can find crystal clear water, so we know it is beautiful and inviting. Trees on either side of a river are quite common, but the *"tree of life" (same tree as in Genesis 2:9) is described as one tree, but on either side of the river. Wow! How can that be? Can you visualize a crystal-clear river flowing under the trunk of the tree with its massive branches flowing out and above? The huge Sequoias and Redwoods that grow in California could possibly be comparable.

The first verse of Genesis states, *in the beginning God created the heavens and the earth.* With these words He is referring to the sky and the heavenly bodies - the sun, moon, stars, and planets. But this is not "Heaven" the eternal home God has prepared for all believers. Heaven, the place, is more often referred to in Scripture as a Kingdom or House, prepared for believers.

Examples from Scripture:

surely goodness and love will follow me all the days of my life, and I will dwell in the **house of the Lord** *forever.* (Psalm 23: 6)

Blessed are the poor in spirit, for theirs is the **kingdom of heaven**. (Matthew 5:3)

Blessed are those who are persecuted because of righteousness, for theirs is the **kingdom of heaven**. (Matthew 5:10)

The Lord will rescue me from every evil attack and will bring me safely to his **heavenly kingdom**. (2 Timothy 4:18)

*"As the tree of life grows from both sides of the river, eternal life grows forever from grace. At Eden God placed Cherubim and a flaming sword flashing back and forth to guard the way to the tree of life (Gen. 3:34). But in heaven we will again have access to this tree." (The Peoples Bible, Revelation)

WHERE IS HEAVEN?

We tend to think of Heaven as being above us. The book of Acts describes the events after Jesus ascension - *he was taken **up** before their very eyes, and a cloud hid him from their sight. They were looking intently **up** into the sky as he was going, when two men dressed in white stood beside them. `Men of Galilee,' they said, 'why do you stand here looking into the sky? This same Jesus, who has been taken from you into heaven, will come back in the same way you have seen him go into heaven'* (Acts 1: 9-11).

Jesus' description of judgment day also states, *they will see the Son of Man coming on the clouds of the sky...* (Matthew 24:30). We therefore picture Jesus coming back to us from above and think of heaven as being above the earth.

In answer to the second question, "where is heaven?" – we simply do not know because God doesn't tell us.

We could safely assume that it is another dimension which we cannot see with our human eyes. It is likely all around us.

God has given humans physical bodies and placed us in a three-dimensional world (height, depth, width). He does not give us the ability to see or comprehend anything beyond that. Although we can't know for certain where heaven is, it is comforting to think of our loved ones in heaven as being close by even though we are not able to see or touch them.

Our loved ones -
near, but yet so far...

HOW DO WE GET TO HEAVEN?

As I watched the ABC news special about heaven and listened to statements made by Catholic Priests, Christian Pastors, and Jewish Rabbis, I heard many opinions, but all were disappointing. Of all these men and women theologians who have supposedly studied Scripture extensively, only one spoke up with the truth and that was Evangelical Joel Olsteen. He stated (although hesitantly), "we are saved through faith in Jesus". He was correct.

The truth is amazingly simple. We are saved by God's grace through faith in His one and only Son Jesus Christ. It seems that in all their years of study and time spent in God's Word, these teachers missed the point completely.

Many discussed how one must be a good person - reaching out and helping others, be a good citizen, do not break the law, go to church, etc. But I ask you, *how good is* "good"? There is no human who is perfect. How does one know when "good" is good enough? God expects perfection. He tells us, *be holy because I, the Lord your God, am holy* (Leviticus 19:2). Sin is sin and it doesn't matter what the sin is, it condemns us in God's eyes. We are told in Romans 6:23, **the wages of sin is death.**

You may have never murdered anyone or robbed a bank, but because of that little lie you told, the gossip you shared about someone, that evil thought or hatred you felt in your heart toward another human, or the lust you felt toward someone you were not married to, you stand condemned in God's eyes. So, if that is the case, how does anyone get to heaven?

It comes down to that one little Bible verse we all know so well, but yet take for granted, *for God so loved the world that he gave his one and only Son, that whoever believes in him shall not perish but have eternal life. Whoever believes in him is not condemned, but whoever does not believe stands condemned already because he has not believed in the name of God's one and only Son* (John 3:16, 18). It does not get any clearer than that.

We inherit sin from our parents and their parents before them all the way back to Adam and Eve, the first people God created. Humans cannot obey God's law perfectly. But Jesus did it for us. He lived the perfect life that humans, because of their sinful nature, are unable to live. Out of love for us He chose to suffer and die in our place. He took the punishment we deserve for our sin upon Himself and gave us His holiness. In doing so He paid our debt to God. His blood, shed on the cross for us, washed us clean and made us fit to stand before a holy God. Plainly stated, we attain heaven through faith in Jesus who made us holy by His blood, shed on the cross for our sins. Re-read that verse from John 3:16, 18.

WILL ALL PEOPLE GO TO HEAVEN?

The answer is "no". Jesus tells us, *not everyone who says to me, Lord, Lord, will enter the kingdom of heaven* (Matthew 7:21). People may say, "I believe there is a God". But James 2:19 reminds us, *you believe that there is one God – Good! Even the demons believe that – and shudder.* Saying or admitting there is a God is not faith. *Now faith is being sure of what we hope for and certain of what we do not see* (Hebrews 11:1). Please read the whole chapter of Hebrews 11 to get a better picture of what it means to have faith in God.

Only those who sincerely believe in Jesus as their Savior from sin and come to Him with a repentant heart will receive His gift of salvation when their life here on earth is over. *And without faith it is impossible to please God, because anyone who comes to him must believe that he exists and that he rewards those who earnestly seek him* (Hebrews 11:6).

The second half of that verse from Romans 6:23 on page 17 reads, **but the gift of God is eternal life in Christ Jesus our Lord.** Salvation (heaven) is a gift of God's grace through faith in Jesus, His one and only Son. The apostle Paul tells us, *For it is by grace you have been saved, through faith – and this not from yourselves, it is the gift of God – not by works, so that no one can boast* (Ephesians 2:8, 9).

The word **grace** means **undeserved love.** God, by grace, loves us even though we do not deserve it. He loves all people, even those who do not profess loving Him. He wants all people to receive His gift, but those who reject Him will not receive it. *This is good and pleases God our Savior who wants all men to be saved and to come to a knowledge of the truth* (1 Timothy 2:3,4).

Heaven therefore, is a gift rewarded to all who by faith believe in Jesus, God's one and only Son, as their Savior from sin. Jesus is God in human flesh. He came to earth and lived the perfect and sinless life we are unable to live because of our sinful human nature, and He suffered and died in our place so that we can live forever with Him in heaven.

Sadly, not everyone will go to heaven when they die. God's gift of grace is for all people, but only those who die in faith will receive it.

The Holy Spirit puts faith in our hearts through baptism and through hearing, reading, and studying the Word. *Consequently, faith comes from hearing the message, and the message is heard through the word of Christ* (Romans 10:17).

God's Word, The Bible

If you don't know Jesus and are unfamiliar with God's Word, grab a Bible and begin reading. I recommend the NIV (New International Version) but others are good also. There is much in Scripture which may be difficult for you to understand, but what you need to know for your salvation is clearly written so that even a child can understand it.

The Bible is made up of 66 different books. The first books of the Old Testament beginning with Genesis tell us how God created the world and the first people, how the first people fell into sin, and the promise of a Savior. The New Testament tells us the life-giving Gospel message, which is the Good News of how Jesus, that promised Savior, came to rescue sinners from eternal death.

The Bible is God's story of the history of the world. When you separate the word "History", it reads, "His-Story". It is God's story from beginning to end.

The end has not yet come, but He tells us what to expect and His Word is always true, and it is final. The end will come in His good time. Jesus' resurrection from the dead is our hope for eternity. He tells us, *I am the resurrection and the life. He who believes in me will live, even though he dies; and whoever lives and believes in me will never die* (John 11: 25, 26). Only through faith in Jesus will we see heaven.

The ABC News Special, "Heaven – Where is it and how do we get there?" completely missed the point. It offered no hope for those who were/are searching for answers. Rather than listen to peoples' contrived ideas about heaven, go to God's Word for the answers. He tells us everything we need to know regarding heaven and how to get there.

HELL

The last few minutes of the documentary were a discussion of Hell. God tells us about Hell in His Word also. Many people feel that there is no Hell. To these people I would respond with, "if there is no Hell, then why would Jesus choose to suffer and die for the sins of all people?" Romans 5:8 reads, *But God demonstrates his own love for us in this: while we were still sinners, Christ died for us.* Yes, there is a Hell and it is not a place anyone would knowingly choose to go to.

God is the source of all goodness, light, and love. Here on earth He is present for those who love Him as well as those who do not. But those in Hell will be completely separated from God and from all that is good. There will be no light – only utter suffocating darkness. There will be no laughter or love. Jesus warns, *if your hand causes you to sin, cut it off. It is better for you to enter life maimed than with two hands to go into hell, where the fire never goes out...* [where] *their worm does not die, and the fire is not quenched. Everyone will be salted with fire* (Mark 9:43, 48, 49).

But don't despair thinking you can never be good enough for God. God loves you. Jesus died for your sins. You are His. We are all sinners and without Jesus none of us can ever be good enough for God, but with Him in our hearts and our lives our sins are covered. *...and the blood of Jesus, his Son, purifies us from all sin* (1 John 1:7). He already knows you personally and longs for you to come to Him in faith. Jesus tells us, *Ask and it will be given to you; seek and you will find; knock and the door will be opened to you. For everyone who asks receives; he who seeks finds; and to him who knocks, the door will be opened* (Matthew 7: 7, 8).

You have been washed in the blood of Jesus which brings eternal life. You will not need to fear death or judgment day. Through faith you are "covered in the blood of the Lamb" and you are fit to stand before a holy God. *For [through faith in Jesus] you died [to sin] and your life is now hidden with Christ in God. When Christ who is your life, appears, then you also will appear with him in glory* (Colossians 3: 3, 4). You can be confident that there is an eternal home for you with Jesus in heaven.

Yes, heaven is a real place. It is a beautiful place. I am confident that I will see it for myself when my life here on earth is over because I believe that Jesus, the perfect Son of God lived and died for me. He promises all who believe in Him: *because I live, you also will live* (John 14:19).

I am confident also that I will be reunited there with family members and friends who have died in the faith and gone before me and that I will recognize them. We will eat and enjoy many of the things we have enjoyed in this life, but our lives will no longer be tainted by sin. *He will wipe every tear from their eyes. There will be no more death or mourning or crying or pain, for the old order of things has passed away* (Revelation 21:4).

God will have work for us to do, but it will be a joy to serve Him. *Therefore, they* [believers/saints] *are before the throne of God and serve him day and night in his temple* (Revelation 7:15).

Unfortunately, not all people will go to heaven when they die. Those who reject Jesus in this life will not be there. *Whoever believes in the Son has eternal life, but whoever rejects the Son will not see life, for God's wrath remains on him* (John 3:36). Those who reject Jesus will go to Hell.

"Yes, there is a Hell and it is not a place anyone would knowingly choose to go to."

IN SUMMARY

These answers to the important questions I have discussed: "is heaven real? how do we get there? and who gets to go?" are rooted in Scripture. Scripture also seems to reveal that there will be food in heaven, although our glorified bodies will no longer need food to survive.

*Blessed are those who are invited to the wedding **supper** of the Lamb!* (Revelation 19:9)

*On each side of the river stood the tree of life, **bearing twelve crops of fruit*** (Rev. 22:2).

There is no definite or direct reference to the question of animals in heaven. As far as our pets are concerned, I comfort myself with the fact that animals are a part of God's wonderful creation, and whatever He has planned for them is perfect. We also must keep in mind that heaven is a place where all of our needs are met perfectly. All that we need to be happy will be there. There will be nothing that our hearts desire or long for. So, if our pets are not there, we will not miss them.

We will meet God face to face and we will see and know all those who have died in the Lord and gone there before us. We will even recognize those whom we have never met here in this life - men and women of the Bible - Adam and Eve, Noah, Moses, Elijah, Paul, Peter, etc. as revealed at Jesus Transfiguration (Matthew 17: 1-4).

In heaven there will be no marriage. We will all be members of one family, the family of God. Jesus says, *At the resurrection people will neither marry nor be given in marriage; they will be like the angels in heaven* (Matthew 22: 30).

Do we have to be "good" to go to heaven? The answer is "no" because no human can be good enough to stand before a holy God. We enter heaven only through faith in Jesus, God's perfect Son in human flesh who paid the debt of sin which all humans owe to God. He went to the cross for us and He conquered death by rising again. Because of Jesus, death and Satan no longer have power over those who believe and have faith in Him.

As believers in Christ we will strive to do His will and be an example of His love. Rather than being our way to heaven, serving God and others will be a fruit, or the result of our faith in Jesus. Out of love for God we will strive to serve Him and reflect His love to our fellow man. We are sinners, but His cross reminds us that our sins are forgiven, and we are covered in His righteousness. We have been washed in the blood of Jesus. We are forgiven and free to serve God and our fellow man with a joyful heart and without fear.

TRUTH AND COMFORT FROM SCRIPTURE

Job 19: 25-27 - *I know that my Redeemer lives, and that in the end he will stand upon the earth. And after my skin has been destroyed, yet in my flesh I will see God. I myself will see him with my own eyes - I, and not another.*

Acts 7: 55, 56 - *But Stephen, full of the Holy Spirit, looked up to heaven and saw the glory of God, and Jesus standing at the right hand of God. 'Look, he said, I see heaven open and the Son of Man standing at the right hand of God'.*

John 11: 25, 26 - *I am the resurrection and the life. He who believes in me will live, even though he dies; and whoever lives and believes in me will never die.*

John 14: 2, 3 - *In my Father's house are many rooms; if it were not so, I would have told you. I am going there to prepare a place for you. And if I go and prepare a place for you, I will come back and take you to be with me that you also may be where I am.*

Colossians 1: 15-18 - *He* [Jesus] *is the image of the invisible God, the firstborn over all creation. For by him all things were created: things in heaven and on earth, visible and invisible, whether thrones or powers or rulers or authorities; all things were created by him and for him. He is before all things, and in him all things hold together. And he is the head of the body, the church...*

2 Peter 3: 8, 9 - *But do not forget this one thing, dear friends: With the Lord a day is like a thousand years, and a thousand years are like a day. The Lord is not slow in keeping his promise, as some understand slowness. He is patient with you, not wanting anyone to perish, but everyone to come to repentance.*

Revelation 21:1-4 - *Then I saw a new heaven and a new earth, for the first heaven and the first earth had passed away, and there was no longer any sea, I saw the Holy City, the new Jerusalem, coming down out of heaven from God, prepared as a bride beautifully dressed for her husband. And I heard a loud voice from the throne saying, 'Now the dwelling of God is with men, and he will live with them. They will be his people, and God himself will be with them and be their God. He will wipe every tear from their eyes. There will be no more death or mourning or crying or pain, for the old order of things has passed away.*

Revelation 22: 7 - *Behold, I* [Jesus] *am coming soon! Blessed is he who keeps the words of the prophecy in this book.*

Revelation 22:14 - *Blessed are those who wash their robes, that they may have the right to the tree of life and may go through the gates into the city.*

Philippians 1:21 - *For me to live is Christ and to die is gain.*

About the Author

Christine Pocza Backus

I am a self-taught and self-published author who loves the Lord and loves to write. I was born and raised in Michigan.

In the spring of 2016 I moved to the Milwaukee area to be a caregiver for my oldest son (age 40) who had just been diagnosed with terminal brain cancer. God took him to heaven one year later in the spring of 2017. We enjoyed his precious last year on earth together doing lots of fun things. In the process I met my new husband, Andrew (Andy) Backus, a retired Pastor. We are now happily married and living in the city of Franklin, Wisconsin, a suburb southwest of Milwaukee.

My three living children are still in Michigan and I go back to visit several times a year. Michigan will always be "home" to me.

I use my God-given gift of writing to tell people about Jesus. I pray that all who read this book will be blessed. Heaven is a real place! Jesus has promised and His promises never fail. I hope to see all my readers there someday.

Other books written by this author:

A Walk Through the Word:
A collection of devotional writings inspired by life experiences.

Sing Me Home:

A memoir of the life of the author's oldest son, Robert Pocza.

He was diagnosed with terminal brain cancer at age 40 and died a year later at age 41. It is a story of courage and faith, in the face of insurmountable odds.

To purchase additional copies of this book and others written by Christine, go to:

www.blurb.com, click on **Book Store,** and type in the title of the book you are looking for.

CPSIA information can be obtained
at www.ICGtesting.com
Printed in the USA
BVRC090237060723
666786BV00004B/90